The Sky Is Shooting Blue Arrows

MARY BURRITT CHRISTIANSEN POETRY SERIES
Hilda Raz, *Series Editor*

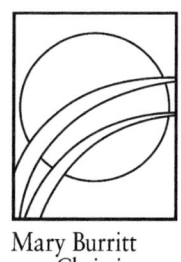

Mary Burritt
Christiansen
Poetry Series

The Mary Burritt Christiansen Poetry Series publishes two to four books a year that engage and give voice to the realities of living, working, and experiencing the West and the Border as places and as metaphors. The purpose of the series is to expand access to, and the audience for, quality poetry, both single volumes and anthologies, that can be used for general reading as well as in classrooms.

Also available in the Mary Burritt Christiansen Poetry Series:

A Selected History of Her Heart: Poems by Carole Simmons Oles
The Goldilocks Zone by Kate Gale
Flirt by Noah Blaustein
Progress on the Subject of Immensity by Leslie Ullman
Losing the Ring in the River by Marge Saiser
Say That by Felecia Caton Garcia
City of Slow Dissolve by John Chávez
Breaths by Eleuterio Santiago-Díaz
Ruins by Margaret Randall
Begging for Vultures: New and Selected Poems, 1994–2009 by Lawrence Welsh

For additional titles in the Mary Burritt Christiansen Poetry Series, please visit unmpress.com.

The Sky
Is Shooting
Blue Arrows

P O E M S

Glenna Luschei

edited by Noel Woodward

University of New Mexico Press • Albuquerque

Library of Congress Cataloging-in-Publication Data

Luschei, Glenna.
  [Poems. Selections]
  The sky is shooting blue arrows : poems / Glenna Luschei ; edited by Noel Woodward.
      pages cm — (Mary Burritt Christiansen poetry series.)
  ISBN 978-0-8263-5493-8 (pbk. : alk. paper
  ISBN 978-0-8263-5494-5 (electronic)
  I. Title.
  PS3562.U75S59 2014
  811'.54—dc23
                        2014001279

Composed in Dante MT Std 11.5/13.5
Display type is Dante MT Std

Cover photograph: *Tres Ocotillos* © 2004 James H. Evans

In memory of Linda Glenn Luschei (1958–1994),
for her namesake Linda Lu Gabriela Luschei,
and for Linda Lu's brother Andrew.

Loving the ritual that keeps me close to you,
Nature tries to keep us apart:

pen, paper, ink, the alphabet,
an orgy for the lonely, longing heart.

—PALLADAS, "LOVING THE RITUAL"
(FOURTH CENTURY AD)

Contents

Part II. Turkish Delight

Part III. Loud and Clear

PART I
The Hunters

Startled to Wake

I smell my grandfather's coffee
and hear the hog futures
on the radio.

I smell the mash
grandmother spread
for the chickens.

It's nearly time to help
her gather the eggs.
It's nearly time to walk
with grandfather
to the post office.
We open the box for letters,
unsettle the hen for chicks.

Now it's time for me
to write letters
to marry to bear
my own children.

It's autumn now.
Amazing to wake
still on this rapturous plane.
Not yet winter.

The Hunters

Sun
crackles over the cottonwood.

The barrel of the rifle
blinds the quail.

Hide from the desert.
Hide in the volcano.

The sky is shooting blue arrows.

Within the arch
we shriek farewell.

Obsidian
obsidian.

Jane over Mountainous Terrain

Thunder out of the Blue
Ridge! Safe in your den we leaned into
the irresistible lightning.
After Stilton, we pressed you
for one last journey:
Greyhound through the South Dakota Badlands,
staking out the New York City bookstore.
You panned for the choice adventure.

Yes! The widowed Victorian invalid
who rode horseback
over the Rockies in sheer aspen light,
boot deep in snow. The black veil over her hat
kept the glare from blinding her.

We see you in a canter, healed
from the pneumonia
that grabbed you in the winter,
cured from weeping tumors that stole
your voice. You are hollering now to the canyons.
Freeee!

At dawn you saddle up.
The martingale's cracked with ice,
but the Appaloosa takes the bit.

You leave behind the corpse at the farmhouse
waiting for burial, and gallop.

Green Parrots

My stepdaughter lives near the green
parrots' roost
high in the eucalyptus.

We crane our necks to catch a glimpse.
Never see, hear them.

She said they fly the coop to join a flock.
Illusion of family.

My stepdaughter weaves on a loom.

Reminds me:
when my hair was waist
long friends braided me into a macramé wall
hanging.

I didn't belong there.

That doesn't mean green parrots don't exist.

On our trajectory North
her father and I searched out the aurora
borealis, never saw it.

Eskimos called the light
"Demon searching out lost souls."

Passing through Sleep

Your voices splash
the mountain of my death

Lover   daughter

Your questions arch
like fish

The Egyptian priest
balances voices

Yours are equal
in sweetness and timbre

You will travel together

I the canyon
sounding echo

Lover   daughter

Leave your dialogue
(volcano and ash)

I cross over
the bridge of a phrase

in no hurry

going to visit Ixtaccihuatl
loved for aeons.

The Tinder Box

You are far away.

States
are crossing blocks
I must step.
Rivers
dogs with copper eyes.

My starving mare
eats
her mane.
The coals are watching us.

Bonfires.
Wigwams.

The Black Hills

1. Landmark

Eyes dark circles
Hubcaps, thermos bottles

The Thoen Stone,
South Dakota:

Came to these hills in 1833
Seven of us. All ded but me Ezra Kind
Killed by Ind beyond the
High hill. Got our gold. June 1834

Got all the gold we could carry
Our ponys all got by Indians
I have lost my gun and nothing
To eat and Indians hunting me

My kids are yelling from the car.
The horizon reels like a telephone wire.

2. Cabin

The cabin isn't mine.
It belongs to the jack pines,
to furious ones
around the fire.

I must be brittle
judging from the mica
I peel from myself.
I must be lichen.

Still I glitter.
Am I gold?
I freeze in an instant,
I must be the harebells.

3. After the Glacier

For days
I heard needles snap
before I felt the chugging
of the cat.

Then the frame houses
their gingerbread
blue horses
the whole village
buckled

and went under.

After the glacier
spruces pop out
on my spine.
Chagall comes back
woodsmen
from Brueghel.

I'm only a filling-station
dinosaur.
My tubes lift
with helium.
Axes flash
and set me free.

The Silver Cross

Alone. I rode the high
mesa. Winds forced me out
to graze with piñones.

Tony. Single, from Truchas
wore the silver cross of Penitentes.
We hunted pine nuts, replaced
them with corn for squirrels.

His place: one room adobe,
bathroom, filthy.
Books lined four walls.

We made love. I went home to fry
tortillas. For Xmas he gave me
turquoise. I gave him the Ouija board.
We never got good as J. M. and D. J.
but the oracle always said

yes.

Before I moved I gave him blue
hyacinth bulbs. Remember
me in spring!

Many springs, mine in trout stream,
his in snow, both hyacinth.

Sprang

I walked out of the prison.
Before the gate clanged
the warden remarked,
"In the Grand Canyon
the rattlesnakes are colored pink
and mauve."

I worked in the desert so long
I envisioned the guards
were no more than saguaro.

No cactus could bleed me.

My antenna snapped.
I didn't hear the viper.

It sprang.

My students said,
"Take a bath in lye.
Grow a tougher hide.
Don't say goodbye. Leave us
with the magic."

Deer

Without ever trying
I find myself a judge.

Spring sounds like deer eating
wins the first grade poetry contest.
Snow falls heavy as a dictionary
comes in second.

I track one of those bucks
fat from a winter of daily rain
and green Manzanita
but no snow at all.

Let the dictionaries fall.
I listen for the deer eating.

Sidewalks

When my children's teeth pushed through with sawtooth edges
I walked crooked sidewalks toward my childhood.

Tragedies walked to meet me. Minor keys strike the songs I sing.

Grandmother lived in Nebraska when
babies died of diphtheria. Afraid to watch her favorite

brown-eyed Caleb go, "Tell me he didn't choke."
Oklahoma children died with dust in their lungs.

Grasshoppers ate the harvest that year. Grandmother stripped
off sheets to cover her cucumber patch.

Families packed up, drove West with nothing but songs.
They survived, left us to tell their stories.

Sleeping In

We had night
work to do, weaving with spiders
hammering back barrel staves.

The family that raised me dozed
long after the collie brought up the paper
after the mailman's retreat.

We worked through tribal
memory: buffalo driven off the cliff
in the Black Hills. Children like us
bundled into bloody carcasses
for warmth.

With the muted voice of owls,
memory spits up pelt.

Women riding to homesteads
in covered wagons
stitched their own shrouds
with their babes' layettes. Today
women with children walk
hours at night to escape amputation.

Children like us in orphanages
learned to hammer coffins for each other.

Guided by Bittern

Guided by bittern
we drove all across Nevada,
Utah, Colorado,
to take out my adored
Aunt Flora on her one hundredth
birthday. We spotted egret
even in the desert.

When we called Aunt Flora
she said "I'll pick you up.
I'm driving a red Cadillac."
Guided by bittern
she drove her daughter
through Mexico
in search of a cancer
cure: the apricot pit.
"When you lose a daughter
you lose one part of yourself.
That was worse than the diphtheria,
the Depression,
the grasshopper plague
when we covered
the wheat field
with quilts."

When I lost a daughter
I gained a self
to drive me
through the flora
the fauna
of the Sonoran desert without a hitch;
through the jimsonweed,
creosote bush.
Over lightning fields to Tucumcari
like the great blue heron

she guides me.

Standing in Line

I am just waiting in my place
behind the others. No shoving.

Will I go gentle like the ones
who went before?

Or will I bolt like the astrologer
who carried his pallet

into the desert on the day
forecast for his death?

Nothing could attack him there
except the swallow that dropped

the fatal pebble on his head.

Feeding Fish by Flashlight

I leave them for the last of my chores
and by the time I finally shake out
their flakes they are no longer hungry,
rising to the top only out of politeness.

"Can't you come back tomorrow, but early?"
they would say. Is procrastination as bad
as pride, presuming we have all the time
in the world, and when we finally arrive

at midnight, knowing our nutrients flow
unheeded over the weir? Or seeing
our children near sleep, eyes half hooded,
still waiting for their story?

Terrycloth

All day I loafed in my house
coat. What a great treat: the bath
robe with its terrycloth lining.
No one looked askance at me
not the doves in the bird
bath.

From my pockets I sowed the sun
flower seeds. By evening I became
St. Francis of Assisi, sowing peace.

Claim

Our families made their marks upon the land.
In Scottsbluff, Nebraska, we saw
the deep imprint of wheel ruts
on the Oregon trail:
chariot wheels
carved into stone at Philippi.

On February 11, 1878,
my grandfather's family
set forth on their prairie-schooner journey
from West Virginia to Nebraska.
When they came to Red Cloud,
they met settlers running back
crying, "Indian raid!"
Great-grandfather John,
unafraid, staked his claim
and made his dugout home.

Retracing these steps,
engravings in the stone,
back to the home in Happy Valley, North
Carolina, where my husband's family lived
for seven generations.

After the Civil War, the brothers, California bound,
shipped their pianos around the cape.
The sisters and the mothers filed to the Pacific
Ocean to do their wash.
They dried long skirts on cypress branches.
Cattle ate the cloth for salt.

Back to the Cave

With Bill in hospital
my dog and I reverted
to Bohemia.
We ordered in Chinese,
licked out the cartons.
Her cookie forecast
great wealth, at least
a jeweled collar.

Every night we went
to the movies,
even got to sit
through the credits.

She deserted her blanket
to jump on my bed,
her brown warmth
a comfort. We forgot
to make the bed.

Second week we reverted
to the cave, gnawed on ribs,
slept on her blanket
before the fire. We all dwell
that close to the cave,
even people in bright
hospitals.

Live Oak Forest

Every morning of our lives I squeezed
your hand and you squeezed back.
Because I stole you I had to check
that you were there.

When we explored the magic forest
I feared for angry tribes.
They would sever my hand.
That's what they do to thieves.

Once you lived in that desiccated
forest of the oak
moth. We brought the leaves to luster,
the butterflies to monarchy.

That night when I hydroplaned to the hospital
I feared to squeeze your hand.
You might squeeze back. I might steal you
and condemn us to eternal flight.

But you were still beneath the muslin sheet.
When they pulled it from your face I adored
your warm freckled shoulders
as I always did, your oaken scent.

Linda Lu's Moonwalk Dream

It's okay to kick the moon when you are four
before the tides gather you in. That moon

that billows into your dream, bigger and bigger
just to let you know it's there. Don't forget.

Good news for me that you stumble through
the craters in your red boots. I will go on.

Now that you kicked the moon,
it knows that you can oppose its control

but later you must surrender
to impregnation. Not a blade of green here

but the tree of life with its eternity of moons
already buds inside you.

That time I flew with your dad on the light
plane over the Grand Canyon right into the Temple

of Vishnu, we learned that we are no strangers
to craters, that beauty comes from hardscrabble.

Regeneration comes from the sterile gravel beds.
You are a princess, but every maharani

must battle for her passion, whether on the moon
or Kashmir. No more kicking. No fooling. It's tough.

You will have no life of your own but the life
of all captivity. I give thanks for those sturdy

kicking legs that join the Race.

Pruning

Twenty-inch pruning saw
(first tool I ever bought)
to coax my *Ceanothus* into shape.
You could call this tool
the new-moon scimitar of Isis.

Eleven years of winter rain
I've been growing a bramble
with California lilac.

Is a formal garden now in order?
I'm willing to submit
to pruning or to wildness.

Clouds of Cambodia

Clouds dwell like lovers over the Mekong River
We walk barefoot through the jungle, splash
through the streets.

I have no lover.

The humidity drowns me into a new life.
I bathe in water from the Mekong and shear
my long hair. The air fills with water
and the river changes course.

It is my time to be reborn, to take refuge as a crone,
to sweep the Buddhist temple with a broom
made of twigs.

In a cascade of rain we study the carving
of creation, how the two armies pull
at Naga, the snake, until the sea churns in milk
and all creatures are born beneath it.

Grip

Your hand slips
from mine like a salmon.
Love of my life
where is your run?
Is our course finished
now that our spawn is done?

Love of my life
death never loses a fish
but where is it taking us now
you upstream and me
down?

When I wake up
with sand in my wrist
I know
I've crept again to the sea
searching for your hand.

Resurrection of Wildness

Thoreau said human nature
adores wildness. Maybe we lose it when we grow
up, but in my waking from that dream fragment you
were saying, "You are wild. There is a frightened bird
beating in your throat."

In my dream as a young woman,
a seer appeared before me with his eyes crossed out.
He asked, "Why have you killed me?"

Leaving It All Behind

Ripped meniscus in my knee
I climb to reach the reclining Buddha and pray
for his blessing, "Let me settle my husband's estate."
I trudge three miles to the top of Penang Mountain
through the open market
where travelers buy silk, T-shirts, and Buddha figurines
to get to the real thing.

I limp up through the painted pagodas,
through the thousand Buddhas to reach
the one and only reclining Buddha. No heart
to slay him on this path but I prayed before the three
statues of Kwan Yin, Goddess of Mercy, my three step
daughters would grant me forgiveness and grace.

I hit the gong and everyone jumped. BONNG!

In Thailand my Buddhist Temple guide
reads my fortune once in Thai and then in Chinese
to make sure it isn't as bad as she thinks:
If you lose something you won't get it back.
If you are ill, it will take you a long time to get well.
"Leave it here," she says. We tie it to the lime tree.

Same in Japan at the Temple of Washing Money.
I did everything right, poured water over my head,
wafted enough incense to make everyone cough.

The fortune-teller made me choose three sticks before I got
one he dared to read for me. Still not great.

That's all right. I accept my destiny. I accept that all is illusion,
everything vanishes. When I left the temple,
even my shoes had disappeared.

Moon Rising

Back from Yosemite
where the moon suffered
a total eclipse on the solstice.

We first suspected its rising was a fire
and turned on the radio

but it peeled back the mountain layers
to bare the persimmon core, bright
orb on winter branches.

The moon towed us home where my family
let me off at my mountaintop house.

When Linda discovered I lived here alone
now since Vavoo died
she said, "The moon can keep you company,"

and it has for us each century,
waxing, waning my eighty years, roundup
of the rabbit.

In one of Linda's dreams she kicked the moon.
"But now we are friends."

Headstone

touch you and Asia at the same moment

—ROBINSON JEFFERS

We rest in peace, in eternal light
on a knoll about the avocado orchard.
We overlook the Pacific, you in black
granite, I in white marble.

Our ashes left before us.
Who said we couldn't fly?

Epilogue

The Willowas stretch out today, spirit
in the sky. Mergansers circle the shore.
Everything takes wing on this autumn dawn.

We guide the drift boat to your favorite
riffle, let your ashes go,
let you go,
swiftly turn.
The osprey takes a dive, catches a trout.

A Near Country

I imagine that country
driven by pain through red rock,
the canyons in Utah.

But in Theresa's first dream
about Bill he was restored
and happy in a white city
that reminded her of Greece.

We were all there
as on our whitewater raft
or in the drift boat steelhead fishing
on the Rogue River,
the only place in this country
where the myrtle tree grows

or the time we came upon the beached
whale on our hike over Big Sur.
TV interviewed Bill
about that whale on his eightieth.

This time in the white city
our first family reunion in the afterlife.

Passage

Now that I am old
and can't find that turquoise pin
or Jemez scarf
I wonder if Spirit is stealing from me
to ease my entrance into the grave.

I want to go simply

in the muslin shroud I cut
when I sewed my baby's layette.
I did not know if I would survive childbirth.
As it was, she died before me.

Still, I want to go simply without
my treasures. Who wants to spend
eternity in King Tut's tomb!

Love Belongs to the West

Love belongs to the north.

—TOM MCGRATH

I see your point, Tom.
The North with its Pole Star
makes us forever faithful, a good trait
in a lover.

I should have known that I was destined
for passion. It took a long time
for a Methodist like me

but I have to acknowledge and welcome
the parade of lovers:
Texas steelworkers and the trapeze artist
who looks great in tights.

The West with its shifting sand.

You don't know what love is
until you've seen the sun set in the West;
sometimes even a green flash
from a poet I want you to meet: Nizar.

PART II
Turkish Delight

Fifty Years on the Road to Love

—FROM A POEM BY NIZAR QABANNI

Nizar, you teach me
that love is not guilt. I thought
it was wrong of me to love him.
We were not equal.

I was free.
He was a prisoner.
You remind me: we are all prisoners.
Love is our jailbreak.

In the mornings he asks me to disrobe
and pass before him.
Oh for the sunny dawns of the desert
when I can go naked on the sand.

Fifty years on the road to love.
I took a detour. Contracts, lawyers.
They are the opposite of love
but no one can get through life
without some business.

Gratitude for My Camel

Thank you, Nizar, for my camel Ma Bouche.

I rode him to the watering hole
an oasis of salt cedar and palm trees.

I know the meaning of his name: my mouth
laughs while my eyes weep

and in Arabic:

the soul laughs while the heart
cries.

He knelt to drink
while I swam.

You and Ma Bouche understand me,
how I can laugh and weep at the same time.

Silence

I used to be jealous, Nizar.
The other one was younger
with black hair
and didn't wear hearing aids.

Now silence is a blessing
I don't have to hear him read
the *Rubiyat* to her.
What a bore.

He doesn't have to read to me either.
I can still hear the faithful
mourning doves who mate
for life.

I would rather read your poems, Nizar,
in silence.

Fretting

You take life too seriously, Nizar tells me.
Fret, fret, over things that can't be helped.

You talk free, free
yet you give in to worry.

Give in to love instead
so people don't think you're a hypocrite.

Turkish Delight

Oh, Nizar, some people call me
lazy, but don't you have to be somewhat
lazy to be a good lover, forget
your schedule, arrive late

from your mint tea and Turkish Delight?
Most important is the long siesta
after fruit and yoghurt, the baguette
still not stale from morning coffee.

One lovemaking after another:
that's the schedule to keep.

Getting Old

And now, Nizar, we have to deal
with getting old
while the soul is always young.

People say, "It's time to give up on love.
Live with your memories."

Never!

PART III
Loud and Clear

Hide from the Desert

Rain hits the windshield in badger print.
Badger, old Medicine Man, you taught me to root.
Stout of heart, mild of will,
orphan brother of the bear,

you leave me off at Raton Pass. I shed this hide
from the desert and take myself

to California.

Blessing of the New Fountain

In Mexico the first man was corn. We forget
the first woman of America was water.
How did we let her slip through our fingers?

How unmindful we were when she bathed
and gave us drink. She was our mother.
We never whispered, "Thank you."

With this new fountain, we beg, "Forgive us."
Thank you, mother, you who taught Helen Keller
to read, you who poured all our elements

into our hands. Bless us and the ones we love.

Year of the Tiger

You stayed here to protect
me from danger.

Peace. I stretched out alongside you,
fingers deep in your ruff.

They say when you bury a tiger
his stripes and bone turn to amber.

I wear the amber neck plate
you gave me. You are there in the claw
and the fleck.

Comings and Goings

In Tucson
when a university student
goes home
she might leave her desk
and a chair, a bookcase outside her cave
with a sign, "Take me."

And who could resist
heat radiating over furniture
like a mirage? You hoist
an old Victrola into your pickup
and ratchet up a new song.

You start that life in the West,
invent a past, and when that tune
winds down, it's okay to put out,
"Take me."

What do we have in life
but comings and goings?

Every Bookcase Can Invent

a vocabulary and a history
like this one.
Craftsmen take note:
tools of the trade:
Plinth, scribe, bay.

My darling had it built
for my seventy-fifth.
Plinth, bay, scribe.
Died before the varnish dried.

Love letters my mother wrote
my father when she left Iowa
for Tombstone, Arizona.
She could not marry a man
divorced, whose wife ran away
when the baby died.
Plinth, bay, scribe.

She wrote, "The sky is shooting
blue arrows across the desert."
She found her freedom in the West
but love pierced her heart.
She took the train to Santa Fe
and crossed the river at last.
Four years later I was born.
Plinth, scribe, bay.

My mother pointed me back West.

Loud and Clear

The hearing-aid man drove up our rutted road, a diplomat
from far away. He carried an attaché case, wore a Panama hat
and a suit. Never mind the August heat.
He was elegant.

Hot, hot, but we shoved corncobs into the cast-
iron stove. Grandmother baked her angel food cake.
"Don't fight, or the cake will fall."

We helped grandfather hitch up
Dixie for the ride to the icehouse, helped him lift
the block with tongs. Ice melted on us all the way home.
We stirred iced tea with mint.

I stood close to grandmother for the test.
The hearing-aid man unwrapped each device from felt,
draped it around her neck.
She held one out to me that looked like a church.
"Can you hear me, grandmother?" I bellowed. "I love you."

That night a storm swept the plains. The light-
ning rods crackled. Grandmother said, "I heard
water."

Now I wear a hearing aid
shaped like the island of Cuba. The voices shout,
"Take my hand. Lift
me out. Don't let me drown alone." I grab
the hands and say "I love you" as I said to grandmother.
I can't turn the voices off.

West to Gain Our Freedom

For Anita Segalman

We grew up on the Missouri
     went on forbidden dates to Sioux City
to a roadhouse where they played "Blue Moon."

We heard Gene Krupa and Harry James when they were young.
I didn't know how beautiful they sounded.

On Highway 75 Floyd Monument stood,
an obelisk to honor the dead with Lewis and Clark.
We drove up the cliff to neck.

Blocks after we crossed the bridge
the granite legend of the city auditorium read
     Art at its truest
     Nature at its finest   are one.

Life was so rich; the loess was rich.   My love
returns to haunt me. We sketched the canyon   the river
and the bluffs. He took me to the beaux arts ball
dressed as devil   I as angel.   There I met Anita.

I married   moved out.
The freeway plowed through my Victorian childhood house.

Ten years later: El Paso, Texas,
and a house with no   basement   closets   attic
We moved West to gain our freedom.
Anita's family settles in the same development.

We plant weeping mulberry   trade sod patches
of Bermuda grass.   Anita invites me to the Seder Feast.
Horseradish on the plates: take the bitter with the sweet.

Every night Anita walks me home.   I turn around
and walk her home.
We had forgotten one another.

Anita and I meet David in El Paso.
He leads us on hikes to the volcano   invites us for magnolia
juleps at the Juarez bar with the marimba.

It kills me to sell my house.   Anita and I
stand in my empty bedroom   light in every corner.

Next stop: the three of us in California.

The Ghost in the DH Lawrence Ranch

I lived there alone.

When I walked down the road through the chamisa and sage,
I paused at the door to let
the ghosts back into their bedrooms.

I never saw them but heard querulous DH scold
Frieda. She and my grandmother, both merry Leos, were matches
for their Virgo husbands. The day of the accident
in the Model T, I was five and remember grandfather
asking her if she was wearing her bloomers
(in case of the hospital). She said, "No, it's too hot."

Frieda said, "Get off it, DH," the time when their car
broke down and he told her not to ride
Tony Luhan's horse back to Taos. DH Lawrence wrote

Women in Love but I was just a young poet
scared of the vapors surrounding me, who tried to invite
real humans to dinner. The ghost told me to defrost
the refrigerator. It got after me for not writing.
Who was this ghost?

DH Lawrence was for life and I loved every minute
of my fearful life.

When I cooked dinner for Frank Waters and Tally Richards,
Frank said I brought images from outer and inner space.
Tally said, "Instead of 'Letter to the North,' you should write
'Letter to the South.'" Took me twenty years to do that.

She called me repressed. I was just scared of the ghost.
At the end of the summer I left.

Green Corn Songs

1.

Bird's nest
knuckle of the birch.
Below
the dandelion, the earthworm.

Trees in the bark of raccoon:
we've grown in our rings.
Moths burst from branches
before I'm ready: green dust
against my face.

Meet me in ancient Puye.
Dwell with me on ledges.
Wind jangles the keys.

Yeast rising in the moon
wind jangles to sleep.

2.

Poetry from Acoma is eggshell white.
Sunflower seeds make a blue slip
the color I am at the root.

Gibbous moon a beehive
stars swarm in November.
Pond has sealed a nest.

I dream of the corn in the winter.

Cumulus

Skies like this make me feel
I could live forever
but no one else ever did.

Clear Coat

All morning my neighbor's sander kept
me from my work.

Buzz, buzz.

I step out and finger the splintery, raw
banister.

A blessing.

How long did it take to get
gummy, corroded? How long did it take
me?

My neighbor said the redwood oil seeps up
from underneath
after a tree has turned to plank

Clear coat is the next step
but I am grateful for one moment with new flesh

for a neighbor who can sandblast.

The Immensity of the Rio Grande

Sprouting up in Colorado, the Rio Grande carried me down
to my first home: El Paso, Texas. It rose East, drew me West.

This Great Heritage River in its immensity dissolves my salty tear.
My first home smelled of compost.
Five times a day I watered the Bermuda grass.
When I pulled out the crab grass invader
at the end of its legs I found a clot.

I pulled my daughter into the desert before the doctor got there.
He would not come until he finished dinner.

My legs filled with clots. I gardened from a wheelchair.
I cried a bitter tear which fell
into the Rio Grande.

Then the River took me North. Las Cruces, Santa Fe.
In the White Sands Missile Range
I held out a cup for water to remember the anguish
of my cousin who perished in the Bataan Death March.

In the reenactment there I cried a salty tear. The Rio Grande
dissolved my hurt.

Walking the Galisteo labyrinth in dust and light
I give thanks that I survived, stride on my own two feet.
Let me embrace my fate,
grant me forgiveness as immense as the labyrinth, the Rio Grande.

From the DH Lawrence Ranch:
The bridge across the River a thermometer. I take my temperature.
I cherish all, forgive all, praise the River.

My Father and Ava Gardner

My mother played piano for the golden silent
movies in Tombstone, Arizona, where she taught
school by day. That was before air conditioning and at night
they would sometimes wheel the piano outside where people sat
on picnic benches with their feet in brittle bush, Rudolph Valentino
projected on the side of the Giant Pawn Shop.
Not so many women swooned on the picnic benches as in the aisles
    inside,
but August 23, 1926, when Rudolph died, women fainted dead away.

My breadwinning father adored Ava Gardner, who looked like my
    mother.
I visited the Ava Gardner Museum in North Carolina and ogled
her voluptuous photographs with her string of lovers, but it wasn't
    until I lost
both of them that my parents' own film played through my heart.

When I was young I never understood my mother's abrupt
departure from Tombstone, Arizona, canceling her contract
for the new school year and all. Was it Rudolph? Could my mother
be the legendary Woman in Black
who visited his tomb at the Hollywood Forever Cemetery?
She was beautiful, like Ava Gardner, and had to stop
in Los Angeles on the way back to Nebraska. She wore black
and could have found her way there to offer brittle bush.

When I was forty and divorced, my brother told me that it was not
    Rudolph
but my father who was the grand hero in her life. Her parents forbade
her to marry him because he was divorced. She left for Arizona.

It was a scandal. My father's first wife left him after the death of their
    baby girl.
She ran away with the doctor. My mother
like Ava Gardner flew back to marry the man she loved.
When my brother shared their romance he said, "Your life can be
    good
after a divorce," and it is.

When my brother gave me her lost valise from Tombstone, Arizona,
I found the Western Union telegrams from my father, "I love you.
    Stop."
"Come back to me now or I will ride to capture you. Stop."
"I will carry you off. Stop."

Tragedy Plums

We left Four Corners, our breakfast
Navajo fry bread.

New Mexico, Arizona. At the border
the highway patrol gave us a ticket.

Linda wrote my mom a postcard,
"California is the police state."

We wore bellbottoms
and miniskirts.

Everything different: palm trees,
carpeted grocery stores.

We found a glamorous fruit
called Tragedy plum.

It was the week of the Sharon
Tate murders.

Tragedy then, always tragedy.
We could still walk in beauty.

Watermelons

Now you watermelons
when thieves come
pretend that you are frogs
—BASHO

While our boys fought in France, braceros came North to work
the fields. When mother heard they had only a cot
she took sheets and blankets to their camp.

A man she knew pulled his wagon along our street.
"*Sandías, sandías,*" he called. Mother spoke
to him in Spanish. One oblong watermelon looked like a submarine.

We could see U-boats plowing up the Missouri. Men built
a tower in my Iowa neighborhood to spot the zeros from Japan.
My father was the air-raid warden and climbed the tower

when the sirens blew. We lay scared in bed until he called,
"All clear, all clear," so we could turn on the light.

"*El corazón,*" the bracero said and plunged his machete deep
into the heart of the submarine melon. He speared the most
delicious dripping wedge I have ever tasted in my life

or ever will taste.
I could spit out the seeds.

"Say *gracias,*" said mother and gave him the quarter he asked
for the melon.

Later when I moved my own family to Albuquerque, their
    neighborhood
was different from mine: Vietnam protests in the street. Our first
    night
someone stole Erich's bike.

Sunset, we drove into the red, red heart of the Sandia Mountains.
No watermelons in Sandia Pueblo. "Green reed place" was their
ancient
name, a good thing in the desert. We bought watermelon from
Safeway.

Creosote People

I lost my wedding ring in the desert, digging up lechuguilla for my rock garden.

Free, at last.

I spent a long time hunting rocks in El Paso. They multiplied again at night, growing out of each other, like hydras.

The odor of night is the greasewood, oldest plant in the world. It gives us hope that even standing so far apart from the others, we survive and connect.

Our roots entrenched in the West branch out for water. When it rains our fragrance fills the desert. People ask why we are independent, not touching. We take only the space that we need, touch underground at the root.

Elephant Butte

The wind races its motor over Elephant Butte
I remember the water pipe
we fought over, dividing furniture.

Then I wanted everything. Now I want nothing.
Whatever it is, take it with my blessing.

I learned the language of the plant,
the stone. Things are not as they seem.

The wind helps me distribute
my riches, steals my gloves, my scarf
even my hearing aid.

People drown here.
I wake to one more blustery day, a safe boat
ride back to the camper.

Potsherd

Mornings he cooked me porridge
from steel-cut oats. While he stirred
I drank latte.

When I found out
his middle name was Carthage
(ancient Phoenician port)

I fell in love.

Suppers I warmed up enchiladas
my housekeeper made.
I wasn't into cooking.

I began to lose things, amethyst

earring in his bed, library book
in the movie, my scarf
from the British Museum.

I could sense I was about to break
camp, smash the bean pot,
move on.

He said it first, "I'm gone."

He left his es-
presso machine in my kitchen,
Model XP 1020 Krups.

Angels / Albuquerque

Albuquerque Heights. Good for bike
riding on Alvarado St. One night the park
sprinklers caught me. I rode
through the spray, my own rain dance.

I rode my little boy to Albuquerque preschool co-op.
The spokes trapped his foot.
A man rushed out on Alvarado St.
He grabbed my son.

I confessed to my therapist: *I was careless.*

That night I dreamed my therapist gave me a bracelet
like the hospital ones my new babies wore.
I said, "You delivered me."
He said, "Sometimes babies are cold
and wet."

I rode my bike. *Free.*

I took sopaipillas and honey to Alvarado St.
but I could never find the man
or even his apartment.

He must have been one of those angels
there for my salvation.
Now and then they appear when I need them most.

My son remembers the white cast
he wore when he was two.

Loving the Dragon

In Australia the Lace Monitor lizard
and I stand toe to toe. His one lunge:
my foot is gone.

There's a secret here I'm trying to get.
I'm back as a child on the Missouri, out for catfish.
Everything muddy here.

West, for steelhead.
My line with caddis fly drifts down translucent
waters to lure the big one.

Things still elude me. I learn from what
I fear. I can love more than the safe
and ceremonial.

This dragon's barbels
so like the catfish,
his appendages make him beautiful.

Monet's Wild Turkeys

They laughed at him. He painted pink
and blue turkeys in the field
before his patron's blue and pink

mansion. People expected the static
water lilies at Giverny, not the turkey.
You can't tell where the turkey or the artist
will go next.

Critics ridiculed Monet's exhibition. He never got
another commission.

It's the same with the poet. Like the turkey she will stick
her neck out.
A flock of us is enough to make
anyone laugh.

But we hope to create art
that will make viewers sigh, beauty
one hundred years later.

Roswell Blog

In Roswell, the porch
of the Lincoln Hotel provides a comfortable spot
in this monsoon. Jail across the street, we wait out
one more jailbreak.

Under a clear sky we visit the alien museum.
Surely aliens landed here. I'll believe anything.
I believe in lightning fields at Tucumcari.

All this splendor because they invited
me to my grandson's graduation at New Mexico
Military Academy. I wore my blue gown.
The colonel asked me to dance.

Buddhism in Bernalillo

I can let go of it all
but I remember how we came here to run
after Sunday dinners in Furr's Cafeteria.
Not a cent extra to my name
but I reached for millionaire's pie.

The children sang, "Go tell Aunt Rhody
the old grey goose is dead."

Grown, gone.
I let go of it all, but still the little girl I lost
the one with the new long front teeth.

Blue Arrows

Albuquerque: up early to meet the milkman
with his four quarts for my children, cottage
cheese and yoghurt for me.

We moved here from a country with sun moist
as the round Colombian cheese
wrapped in a banana leaf.

In Albuquerque the sky is shooting blue
arrows. The milkman tells me he prays
to the petroglyphs as he walks the Galisteo

Labyrinth, oldest in the new world. He says, "I rev
up the gods and they rev me up.
It's a two-way street."

The milkman, my only friend in a new town,
my mother comes to visit. When we take her
to the top of Sandia Peak

she passes out. We discover her low
blood pressure in her days at Lovelace Hospital.
"I liked the Western art," she says.

A year later she is well and we go to the state
fair. Now we have friends. I buy a pot
from Harold Littlebird. He gives me his poem.

My daughter Linda wins a blue ribbon for her painting
and poem. "I am the bicycle. I come along
to brighten the way. I ride away

leaving everybody happy." They all made me
happy: the milkman, my mother, Harold Littlebird,
Linda. They all rode away.

Albuquerque Airport

Soldiers stream into the vaulted Albuquerque airport
lit by luminarias on the roof.
Going home for holidays, going West
for a new life, new hope.
I shake the hands passing by.

Will they be able to forget?
Will they be the New Mexico survivors
of Bataan who return each year to Chimayo
to offer thanks to earth? For now, they return in light.

Orgy (ὄργιον)

To the reader:
Before you get your hopes up let me remind you that in Greek
orgy also means work and that is my job, bending over the steam
iron to make my son Tom presentable for his position back West.

Linda, last day of kindergarten, takes down magnetic
ABCs from the refrigerator along with the cards I sent
from Egypt and Greece. No evidence left that
I once strode across the Arabian sands on a camel.
Nothing left from my brush with pirates in Somalia.

Outside, the orgy of work: men water blast
the house. When we called for an estimate,
how many SUVs would fit
outside? That's how they measure square feet.
How many ironing boards, shaped like King
Tut's sarcophagus, headboard at the top?
How many alligators?

This is Florida, and I want to go home. Ritual: moving back West.

Water blasting, steam iron spurting, my last ditch
stand, final trip. In my obit,
she went out ironing. No mention
of the early day
orgy at all, forgotten as my postcards. A tear splashes the shirt.

Supper a picnic in the bayou: pimento sandwiches, watermelon
pickles, sweet tea. Yasmin sees the moss that shrouds the giant oak
as phantom. All our family dinners turn to talk of the supernatural.
Our guesthouse holds a ghost.
Once Tom's sister Linda appeared above him with a message
before he woke.

We never receive the messages in time.

Our family ritual, takes in work by day,
at night remembers the dead, moves on, back West.

Monsoons in New Mexico

I lose everything, as it's meant to be.
Turquoise pawn slides from my wrist,
silk scarf from my neck.

Monsoons in New Mexico are short
as life. In the arroyos
tadpoles grow instantly to frogs.

Then desert. Everything desert.

How fortunate
I am each dawn to wake up alive.

To the Muse

I know that I have been derelict, joined Facebook
though only for a fortnight.

Oh, Muse, let me return to the freedom of the West
when you and I lived raw, before I left for Lotus Land
and forgot my home. Return me to those days
before my taming when I flew with kingfishers.

Let me become the wonderer I was, in the orgy
of creation, let me beat the snare
drum in my heart, that pulsar that would strike
in the planets from inner and outer space.

Oh, Muse, grant me that second wind where I run
and run and can't think of anything but One,
the race of God and Man.

I don't know who is in front of me or behind me but
grant me the snap of the finish tape across my breast.

Golden Jubilee for Aimee Semple McPherson

Sister Aimee, the first time my mother heard me preach to the
     Methodist
Church she said I could be you
                    evangelist.
She didn't know I also went dancing at forbidden roadhouses.
We adored your theatrical productions at the Four Square
Cathedral: that opera about your plane piloted by the devil.
          It crashed.

As a child you delivered sermons to friends. Me too, even to my cat
and to my canary Richard (which the cat ate).
That cat was driven by Satan. I wrote a play about him.

You played the tambourine in the Salvation Army Band.
In rhythm band they gave me the ocarina.
Thousands came to hear you
          and when you disappeared
into the waves, thousands combed Santa Monica pier for you.
          Two rescuers drowned.

Your mother gave the sermon that next day (I don't know whether
     my mom
would have done that though she did speak
          to my fourth grade class about King Tut)
and announced to the mourners, "Sister is with Jesus."
Everyone screamed and passed out which was good but now comes
     the bad part.

The engineer from your radio show was also gone. I felt guilty.
Mother was afraid I would grow up to run off
with Porfirio Rubirosa.
                    Someone saw the two of you in Carmel.
Later when you stumbled out of the desert, held for ransom by
    Mexicali Rose,
the Press took after you.
From then on they ignored you.
                    Like a movie star you died, at only fifty-three.

I never got to be you, but couldn't I buy the house your faithful built
on Lake Elsinore: Moroccan patterns in the prayer room,
                    Moorish doors?

You built two secret paths and tunnels for escape:
the Press again. Well, Aimee, if I can't be you or even buy your home
    let
me at least march with the Salvation Army Band in the Rose Parade
                    when they play
"Golden Jubilee." Let me shake the tambourine and my booty
        down the whole five and a half miles.

Moonwalk

July 20, 1969

That Albuquerque night
we sat around the black and white
and listened for the crunch
on the moon's crust. All the world was crater.

Ear/earth. I heard the cricket.
We held hands.
I published the first
issue of *Café Solo*, mailed out invoices on white
envelopes with the black moon stamp.

That night of the brave moon
changed everything for us
in our white dream suits.

Our neighbor claimed it was a ruse.
"But," she said, "the moon
still can have a future."

Cellar Door

Cellar door: some say the most
beautiful words in the English language. I say the scariest.
A child, I wrenched open that cellar door
at the abandoned ranch in Abiquiu.
What a racing murder of black
widow spiders I cut
loose, midway through a meal.

Since then, I've read about how ancient
Spiders evolved
in caverns, far back as creation.

We all do what we can.

I slammed the cellar door shut.

Forever,
you might think.

But I came back to crack it open,
to observe the fat white egg sacs arranged like planets
in the web: Mercury, Venus, Mars.

When I grew up I found out that my own Pluto opposite
my moon in Capricorn gave me that make or break chart,
someone who would tempt
the sinister spider but still escape.

Bookcase Blog

Each bookcase can hold a secret
drawer. Mine has one to secure the jade, a present
from Bill.

And on this shelf
my father's humidor. Mother gave him a pipe
but he loved to chew cigars, toss them over the porch.
The other kids and I retrieved and smoked them.

In Cuba I toured a cigar factory, visited the curing house
where tobacco farmers sleep nude to judge
the direction of wind on tobacco leaves. The dark
forest of two-by-fours in my father's lumberyard
where I longed to sleep hot June nights in Iowa.

From the bus, fields of tobacco and sugarcane,
not a vegetable patch in sight:
In early March, my father's turnip patch.

On the magazine rack, *The New Mexican* from Santa Fe.
The Owen Lopez I knew in Bogota retires from the McCune
Foundation. He gave out coins to *chinitos* on the street,
gave out millions for McCune. He said, "I bet
on the jockey, not on the horse." He taught Linda to ride
a horse at the Lee Ranch.

He met us at the train in Santa Rosa. He moved us to New
Mexico.

And last here is Linda's wedding album.
I still don't have the nerve to open it.

Trout Fishing in Montana

The idea is you hunt
the nymphs,
hook them for bait.

I hunt the dragonfly
glorious helicopter
that tells us

once you leave the water
you can never come back.

Solstice

Loving the ritual that keeps me close to you,
Nature tries to keep us apart:

pen, paper, ink, the alphabet,
an orgy for the lonely, longing heart.

—PALLADAS (FOURTH CENTURY AD)

Time for our annual persimmon walk
before the fuyus are claimed by bear
and birds who will not migrate.
Friends arrive, clipper and sack,
move with Druids through the trees.

Missing you, I pray for a healing rite.
Our honeymoon at Stonehenge
light cracked through the rock,
Out of all the sparklers in the observatory I lit
on you, one in a million

million. I'll hike the hill and back
home, take up your job to slice the fruit
down to galaxy then dehydrate
them for an evening snack. That's when my heart
longs most for you.

Walking through the day, I'll meditate.
Late afternoon when friends pack
their bags, seek their way
I'll light the fire and settle in with laptop,
write you of our old life, my new.

Notes

"The Black Hills": The full text of the Thoen Stone in South Dakota reads,

> Came to these hills in 1833
> Seven of us Delacompt, Ezra Kind,
> G. W. Wood, T. Brown, R. Kent,
> Wm King, Indian Crow
> All ded but me Ezra Kind
> Killed by Ind beyond the
> High hill. Got our gold. June 1834
>
> Got all the gold we could carry
> Our ponys all got by Indians
> I have lost my gun and nothing
> To eat and Indians hunting me

"Linda Lu's Moonwalk Dream": Linda Lu is my granddaughter, named after my daughter, Linda Glenn Luschei, who died in the AIDS pandemic when she was at the height of her beauty, at thirty-six. She became an AIDS activist and founded the ongoing organization Women at Risk. There are several references to the two Lindas in these poems.

The Santa Fe artist Susan Kelly has illustrated this poem.

"Headstone" and "Epilogue": These poems, among a number of others, are in honor of my Bill, William Franklin Horton, 1926–2009. He passed in our thirty-third year of marriage. It was a second marriage for both of us.

"Love Belongs to the West," "Fifty Years on the Road to Love," "Gratitude for My Camel," "Silence," "Fretting," "Turkish Delight," and "Getting Old": Nizar Qabbani was born in Damascus in 1923. He is most remembered for his battles against the taboos imposed upon women. I would like to thank Tarek Abichou and his family for hosting my family and me on a camel-riding expedition through the Tunisian sands.

"West to Gain Our Freedom": This poem is for Anita Segalman. We first met in Sioux City, Iowa, and were neighbors in El Paso, Texas. After both of us moved to California, we began a series of artist books of my poems and her linoleum block cuts. The first in our series, *Silk & Barbed Wire*, won a prize from the Rounce & Coffin Club in its Western Books Exhibition of 1987.

"Clear Coat": This poem is for my neighbor Lindsay Alicia Wilcox, who beautifies my house with her sanding and painting skills.

"Creosote People": This poem is for Sara Backer.

"Orgy (ὄργιον)": Orgy in Greek has several meanings: Ritual, muse, second wind, and work.

"Golden Jubilee for Aimee Semple McPherson": Aimee Semple McPherson, also known as Sister Aimee, was an evangelist in the 1920s and 30s. Aimee used progressive media methods, such as radio and movies, to preach gospel. She was a practitioner of faith healing and was involved in a questionable kidnapping.

"Solstice": Palladas was a Greek poet who lived in Alexandria, Egypt. A pagan schoolmaster and epigrammatist living in a Christian society, Palladas is known to have written at least 151 epigrams.

Acknowledgments

I am grateful for the following publications that first selected certain poems included in this manuscript: *Askew*: "Fifty Years on the Road to Love," "Gratitude for My Camel," "Silence," "Fretting," "Turkish Delight," "Getting Old," "Leaving It All Behind," and "Watermelons"; *Back into my Body and New Poems*: "The Hunters," "The Tinder Box," "The Black Hills," and "Passing through Sleep"; *Corners of the Mouth, a Celebration of 30 Years at the San Luis Obispo Poetry Festival*: "Blue Arrows"; *Home Planet News*: "Creosote People"; *if&when*: "Green Parrots," "Angels/Albuquerque," and "Trout Fishing in Montana"; *Leaving It All Behind*: "Leaving It All Behind," "Green Parrots," "The Hunters," "Resurrection of Wildness," "The Black Hills," "Terrycloth," "To the Muse," and "Sleeping In"; *Libido Dreams*: "The Silver Cross," "Passing through Sleep," "Sleeping In," "The Tinder Box," and "Feeding Fish by Flashlight"; *Miramar*: "Moonwalk" and "Buddhism in Bernalillo"; *Matriarch*: "Sprang"; *Pembroke Magazine*: "My Father and Ava Gardner," "Loud and Clear," "Year of the Tiger," "Sleeping In," "Linda Lu's Moonwalk Dream," "Leaving It All Behind," and "Jane over Mountainous Terrain"; *Pianos Around the Cape*: "Grip," "Guided by Bittern," "The Tinder Box," and "Claim"; *Poetry Nook*: "Watermelons"; *The Poet's Domain*: "Cumulus," "Monet's Wild Turkeys," "Orgy," "Loving the Dragon," and "Cellar Door"; *Prairie Schooner*: "The Black Hills"; *Presa*: "Green Corn Songs," "Comings and Goings," and "Solstice"; *San Luis Obispo Tribune*: "Feeding Fish by Flashlight"; *Second Genesis: An Anthology of Contemporary World Poetry*: "Every Bookcase Can Invent," "Elephant Butte," "Bookcase Blog," and "Watermelons"; *Seedpods*: "Feeding Fish by Flashlight"; *Shot with Eros*: "Jane over Mountainous Terrain," "The Tinder Box," and "Passing through Sleep"; *Silk & Barbed Wire*: "West to Gain our Freedom"; *Total Immersion*: "Jane over Mountainous Terrain" and "Blessing of the New Fountain"; *200 New Mexico Poems*: "To the Muse"; *Ventura County Writer's Club Anthology*: "Monsoons in New Mexico"; *Unexpected Grace*: "The Black Hills" and "Sidewalks"; *Witch Dance*: "Clouds of Cambodia," "Linda Lu's Moonwalk Dream," "Headstone," "The Tinder Box," "Pruning," "Passing through Sleep," "Live Oak Forest," "Jane over Mountainous Terrain," "Grip," "Back to the Cave," and "Standing in Line"; *World Poets Quarterly*: "The

Immensity of the Rio Grande," "Clear Coat," and "The Ghost in the DH Lawrence Ranch."

I am also grateful to Elise Muriel McHugh and to Hilda Raz for granting me full reign in writing this book, and to Noel Woodward for her editorial assistance. Heartfelt thanks also go to the Santa Barbara Sunday poets, especially Barry Spacks; the Cambria Writers' Workshop; and to James Ayers for helping me to get it right.